CW00506819

# GETTING
# POSITIVE

take small daily actions,
change the way you feel

Stuart Parkin

Grosvenor House
Publishing Limited

The right of Stuart Parkin to be identified as the author of this
work has been asserted in accordance with Section 78
of the Copyright, Designs and Patents Act 1988

The book cover is copyright to Stuart Parkin

This book is published by
Grosvenor House Publishing Ltd
Link House
140 The Broadway, Tolworth, Surrey, KT6 7HT.
www.grosvenorhousepublishing.co.uk

This book is a work of fiction. Any resemblance to
people or events, past or present, is purely coincidental.

A CIP record for this book
is available from the British Library

ISBN 978-1-83975-482-1

# CONTENTS

Things in our lives do not always go as we would like indeed, in the last year, things have not gone as most people would have planned. This has led to much frustration. When this situation persists over a sustained period, a positive outlook is challenged if not destroyed, we cease to believe what we want to happen, will happen. We cease to show up positively for those around us: Our family, our friends, our colleagues, our clients. You can change how you show up, from now.

This small book is designed to help you rediscover a more positive outlook. The good news is, far from being powerless there are a variety of small actions you can take. This little book shares some of them.

Turn to any page and feel more positive.

"Without us there is no good or bad, only perception. We decide what story we tell ourselves. We decide how we will react." Marcus Aurelius

"There is good in everything, if only we look for it." Laura Wilder

"That doesn't kill me, makes me stronger." Friedrich Nietzsche

"Suffering arises from trying to control what is uncontrollable, or from neglecting what is within our power." Epicetus

"Talking about our problems is our greatest addiction. Break the habit. Talk about your joys." Rita Schiano

"I can be changed by what happens to me, but I refuse to be reduced." Maya Angelou

# Smiling

Smiling releases tension and whether genuine or not, the same positive biological effects are felt in your body. So, fake it more often.

"Love the life you live. Live the life you love."
Bob Marley

# Dance

Let go! Raise your energy, mind and body, rumba, salsa, tango, whatever, dance the night way.

"Some people feel the rain. Others just get wet."
Bob Dylan

# Comfort Food

When all else seems to fail, eat something that provides comfort because of the taste but quite possibly because of its association with good times. This will make you stronger.

"We only live once, but if you do it right, once is enough." Mae West

## Environment

For some, an organized, uncluttered environment makes for an uncluttered and clear mind. Try Feng Shui and see whether this improves how you think.

"Don't go through life. Grow through life."
Eric Butterworth

# Herbal Hope

For centuries herbs have achieved many things including enhancing the flavour of our foods, effective digestion and they have improved the clarity of our thinking. Try saffron or ginseng.

"Act as if what you do makes a difference. It does."
William James

# Memory Bank

Know that when times are more challenging, you are far more likely to cope if you have a body of positive experiences to draw upon. These provide the context for you to see that despite life's' challenges, there have been and will likely be more good times. Build up your memory bank account.

"I have found that if you love life, life will love you back." Arthur Rubenstein

# Mantra

Develop a phrase that you say every day and at every moment when you feel you are losing control. Say this enough and you will begin to believe the mantra.

"Every day, things are getting better." Emile Coue

# Happy days

Let the good times roll. Imagine it is 'that time' of the year. There are certain times of the year we all naturally feel good. It could be your birthday, Christmas Hannukah, Eid Al-Fitr, Diwali or some other celebration which brings a sense of closeness.

"Creativity is intelligence having fun." Albert Einstein

# Innocence

The beauty of innocence, of a toddler taking its' first steps or the exuberance of a bounding puppy, cannot but make for a positive reaction and focus our minds positively.

"Walk on with hope in your heart and you'll never walk alone." Rogers & Hammerstein

# Switch on Switch Off

Lights, computers, and engines can all be switched on and off. Learn what it takes to switch off your mind so that it can recharge. Perhaps a sensory deprivation tank?

"What we fear most is usually what we need to do." Tim Ferris

# Clarity

Uncertainty creates indecision and inaction which over time damages confidence. Wherever possible seek clarity sooner rather than later.

"The best way to predict the future is to create it."
Peter Drucker

# Tone of Voice

Positive people speak with a slow deliberate self-assurance if not belief. To convince others, if not yourself, breathe deeply and speak more slowly, hearing the words you speak.

"Only in the darkness can you see the storm."
Martin Luther King

# Same Old

Patterns and order allow us to function, to not have to think about every detail of everything we do. But equally, 'same old' every day, the opposite of variety, can in time wear down the spirit. So, mix things up. If not a trip, learn a new skill or meet some new people.

"You will face many defeats in your life but never let yourself be defeated." Maya Angelou

# Goal Setting

Positive people are driven often because in the first place they are pursuing experience or outcomes that excite them. Set yourself a challenge that excites you and where the challenge is not your choice, find a reason why overcoming it will make you a stronger, better person.

"Legacy is not leaving something to people, it is leaving something in people." Peter Strople

# Determination

Persistent physical or mental effort directs us away from negativity and toward resolution and achievement. Chose something you are passionate about and do not give up its pursuit. Copy. Paste.

"Stay close to anything that makes you feel glad you are alive." Hafez

# Achievement

When we get things done, we feel good about ourselves, even if they are accomplishments that do not change the world but change the way we feel about the world. Complete something small today such as learning the words of a new song or discovering a new show to watch. Or perhaps, phone a long-lost friend.

"Be kind whenever possible. It is always possible."
Dalai Lama

## Cat Naps

If you can, grab a few minutes to get a few zzzzzzzzz
during the day. You will be surprised how rejuvenating
a quick sleep can be.

"To live without hope is to cease to live."
Fyodor Dostoyevsky

# Hydrate

We all love our coffee/tea, our carbonated drinks and booze, but what they give they steal in terms of hydration. Drink more water and feel your body and mind applaud with appreciation.

"Everything you've ever wanted is on the other side of fear." George Addair

# Hot Tub

For breakthrough thinking which stems from quality relaxation, try a hot tub (or sauna). It worked for one of the ancient worlds' greatest philosophers, Pythagoras.

"Nothing is IMPOSSIBLE. The word itself says 'I'm possible.'" Audrey Hepburn

# Vision

The clearer and/or more compelling our future direction appears, however difficult the path ahead, the more optimistic we are likely to be. Plan to work at or for something you really want.

"Things turn out best for the people who make the best of the way things turn out" John Wooden & "Always look on the bright side of life!" Monty Python/Life of Brian/Eric Idle

# GV20/Bai Hui

Located at the crown of your head is an acupressure
point, GV20, also known as Bai Hui. Gently massage
it, breath deeply and feel a sense of peace.

"You make a life out of what you have, not what
you're missing." Kate Morton

# Avoidance

An endless challenge, a cause you do not believe in,
surrounded by negativity? All these things drain
your energy and will make you less positive.
Avoid such things.

"One's destination is never a place, but a new way of
seeing things." Henry Miller

# Greenify

Make your home and work abundant with plants. Plants pump out oxygen whilst absorbing carbon dioxide. Cleaner air makes for a more resilient and effective mental outlook.

"Get busy living or get busy dying." Steven King

# Stomach it

Be kind to your stomach and your mind will follow.
There is a body of science that suggests that mental
health and gut/stomach health are connected. Eat
foods and drinks that are easier on your stomach.
Try raw foods. Drink mint tea.

"Worry is a misuse of the imagination." Dan Zadra

# Relaxation

To know what relaxation feels like, consciously tense all your muscles tightly for ten seconds and then completely relax them. This will not only help circulation but give you a sense of consciously feeling tensed up and knowing what being relaxed feels like.

"A journey, I reflected, is of no merit unless
it has tested us."
'In Search of King Solomon's Mines.' Tahir Shah

# Hard Work

When you are working hard, your actions will take you closer to your goals and if you are focused, your work will take you a step away from your worries.

"Life is what happens while you're making other plans." Allen Saunders

# Preparation

Preparation makes it easier to be positive.

"I am prepared for the worst but hope for the best"
Benjamin Disraeli

# Head Space

Much of the stress you experience is real for you,
but it is often about things that will never happen.
Understand this and you will develop some protection
from even your worst anxieties. Try talking things
through with someone you trust.

"Some people look for a beautiful place. Others make a
beautiful place." Inayat Khan

# Raw Food Is Hopeful

Our bodies use much of our energy simply to digest food. To minimize how hard your stomach must work and so to free up your problem-solving mind, eat more fruit, beans, nuts, and pulses.

"Once you replace negative thoughts with positive ones, you'll start having positive results" Willie Nelson

# Pattern Breaking

If you have a perfect day, then change nothing. If you
have days when negativity ensues, mix things up.
Go on an adventure or simply change the structure
of your day. Perhaps eat at a different time, walk,
or drive a different route to work, alter what you
read, watch, or listen to.

"When the power of love overcomes the love of power,
the world will know peace." Jimi Hendrix

## Posture

Heads up, when you have great posture, the energy
in your body feels better and so does your confidence.
Slouch and the aches will appear so if standing,
straighten up and if sitting, support your back.

"Have no fear of perfection, you'll never achieve it."
Salvador Dali

# Clear Your Mind

Getting away from a pressurized state of mind is simply achieved by changing your energy. Get up and move around, better still, go outside, and take a walk and breath in some distraction!

"There is nothing impossible to him who will try."
Alexander the Great

# Common Cause

The power of many makes the unattainable that bit closer. Find others confronting or who have confronted the challenge you face. It will feel a little less daunting.

"You'll never find a rainbow if you're looking down."
Charlie Chaplin

# Imagination

Cultivate your ability to see beyond the obvious. If you do this, whatever your reality and however bad it might feel, you will always have the ability to tap into a world that can bolster your spirit.

"Every moment is a fresh beginning" T.S. Eliot

# Baby Steps

Positivity begins with the experience of things going right/working out. Usually these successes are smaller things, they are baby steps to overcoming much larger challenges. See tasks achieved however small, as accomplishments and progression. These smaller accomplishments are the groundwork for positive thinking.

"Oft hope is born when all is forlorn." J.R.R. Tolkien

# Experience

The experience of your life shows you that despite major challenges, that you are still here, that things work out if not resolve. Draw on your experience of positive outcomes and immediate challenges will too pass.

"Let your hopes not your hurts shape your future."
Robert S Schuller

# Good News

If you are going to watch/read the news, limit
how much you watch as it is usually negative.
Counterbalance what you watch/read with positive
things, perhaps a wildlife documentary?

"When you stop hoping you start settling."
Valorie Burton

# Energy

If you have better energy levels, you are much more likely to be able to front up to the world. So, eat well, breath clean air, drink clean water, sleep well and you will have a more positive outlook.

"Let no one ever come to you without leaving happier."
Mother Theresa

# Passions

What we are passionate about we can easily focus our time with enthusiasm, if not joy. This in turn does not allow us to be positive rather, we are in a state of positivity. Spend your time at and away from work on things that mean something to you.

"Would you have an empire. Rule over yourself."
Publilius Syrus

# Dreams

Our dreams are the window to what is possible and what we hope for. While we dream, all things are possible, and we are truly alive. Ensure you get a good nights' sleep.

"Happiness is not the absence of problems, but the ability to deal with them." Charles De Montesquieu

# Routine

Knowing what must be done and when makes for peace of mind but too much routine, too much predictability can drain your energy and impact your state of mind. Have a routine but ensure you continue to stretch yourself on some level too.

"Come what may, all bad fortune is conquered by endurance." Virgil

# Setting Boundaries

Working from home has made the division between working and not, much more blurry. Make a point to ensure non-work time and if possible, non-work spaces. Feel your positivity improve.

"The greater the obstacle the more glory overcoming it." Moliere

# Open Mind

By having an open mind, you can see that most
things are possible but as Carl Sagan quipped, do
not make it too open!

"I think your mind is so open, your brain fell out."
Carl Sagan

# Negativity

Some people for many reasons, are negative all the time. Aim to avoid such people or if you cannot, give them a copy of 'Getting Positive.'

"Nothing is more beautiful than the smile that has struggled through the tears." Demi Lovato

# Feet

To achieve great feats your feet are key. Reflexologists know this. Soaking and massaging your feet and you will be nurturing in turn your whole body.

"People begin to be successful the minute they decide to be." Harvey Mackay

# Opportunity

Learn to see what is amazing all around you.
The brightest colors in nature, the cleansing effect
of driving rain or the variety of dawn birdsong.
See what is wonderful for what it is, and you
will move toward positivity.

"To love beauty is to see light." Victor Hugo

# Strategy for Doubters

If you lack confidence in an outcome, look to similar situations that worked out and so challenge your doubt. If doubt persists, chose consciously either to use your energy to doubt or to focus on doing the best you can. If you chose the latter, you could at least have no regrets.

"In the middle of every difficulty lies opportunity."
Albert Einstein

# Big City Blues

Big cities are never boring but because of that, they can wear you down. Convening with nature is much easier on the eye and on the mind. Get out of town more often.

"The worst enemy to creativity is self-doubt."
Sylvia Plath

# Olfactory Opportunity

Incense burning, fresh flowers or even freshly brewed coffee can all bring a sigh of relief or a smile of appreciation.

"It is not the resources but the resourcefulness that ultimately makes the difference." Tony Robbins

# Growth

When we master new things, we are strengthened
mentally if not physically. Expanding your mind
is a real example of growth. Stagnation is the
opposite and causes negativity.

"The secret of getting ahead is getting started."
Mark Twain

# Worry

There should be few things in your life that make you feel hopeless. Perhaps you feel like this because you are worrying about too many things? If you can focus your energy on one thing that really matters to you, you will be much closer to resolving it and, everything else will feel better.

"Stop looking for angels. Look for angles."
Ryan Holiday

# Perspective

Seeing things in context makes them more understandable. And, what we understand brings us closer to acceptance, if not change. Take a break from your current situation and give yourself a chance to see it for what it is.

"Most of the problems in life are for two reasons: We act without thinking or we keep thinking without acting." Zig Ziglar

# Control Freak

It is never good to be a control freak even with things you know you can control. Worse for your mental state, worrying and trying to control things over which you have no control. Worry about what you can do something about and for the rest, seek support or other ways to manage.

"It is the mark of an educated mind to be able to entertain a thought without accepting it." Aristotle

# Blooming Marvelous

The scent of a rose, of lavender and frangipani, all classic and uplifting. The body responds with serotonin, which in turn relaxes the brain.

"Love cures people – both the ones that give it and the ones who receive it." Karl A. Menninger.

# Massage

It might not cure your mental state, but it will help relax you and provide respite from the pressure you feel.

"If you carry joy in your heart you can heal any moment." Carlos Santana

# Reward Yourself

Especially on a work day, make a point of providing
mini rewards you receive on completing tasks
you've set yourself. This reinforces what
you've achieved apart from the pleasure of
enjoying the reward as well.

"If there is no struggle there is no progress."
Frederick Douglass

# Mind Your Language

Just as what you see and hear can impact how positive you are, your own language can reinforce your negativity. Make a point today to consciously think about the words you use and where negative, to temper them. For instance, "Maybe" for "No.'

"Every human being needs to listen consistently to live fully." Julian Treasure

# Templates

If you want to be more positive, seek templates of positivity. Who in your life is a model of the way you would like things to be/a model of positivity as you see it? Talk with them more often. And find more people like them and read about, listen, and be inspired by them.

"Silence is the sleep that nourishes wisdom."
Francis Bacon

# Industry

If you keep busy performing a task and you are wholeheartedly focused on it, you are in the moment of 'doing'. Negativity does not enter the equation.

"Let yourself be silently drawn by the strange pull of what you really love. It will not lead you astray." Rumi

# Support

Whether the chair you sit on that supports your back
or the loving support of your family around you,
support allows your body and mind to function
so much better, positively disposed to all
challenges. Join a club!

"It's not what you look at that matters, it's what you
see." Henry David Thoreau

# Belief in Ourselves

You show up every day and get through it and
have done that in your life for thousands of days.
There might be challenging times, but back yourself
perhaps taking some knocks, to come through
and others will too.

"A gem cannot be polished without friction, nor a man
perfected without trials." Seneca

# Certainty

A lack of positivity is based on your belief that there is
no possibility of a positive outcome or at least, repeated
experience of negative outcomes. Get into the habit of
pursuing an activity that leads you consistently
to positive outcomes. Playing football with your
four-year old?!

"Hopelessness is a feeling. It is not a fact." Anohni

# Deadlines

Things that drag on, drain us and cause feelings of negativity. Decide that things will be resolved by a certain point and either they will or will not but have a plan to move on a new course. Do this and you will feel progression and be a step away from feeling negative.

"What the caterpillar calls the end of life, the master calls a butterfly." Illusions: Richard Bach

# Calming Diversions

Watching the birds in a birdbath, flapping their wings as they preen themselves is strangely captivating. Listening to Mozart uplifting. Combining ingredients to create a new recipe is fun. Such diversions soothe the brain and spirit.

"You have been criticizing yourself for years, and it hasn't worked. Try praising yourself and see what happens." Isaac Asimov

# Three Rule

Think of your life as falling in to three areas: "H/W/R"
Home, work, and relationships. At any stage of your
life when you feel that two out of three of the "HWR"
are failing, it is likely that you will be vulnerable if
not, negatively inclined. Recognize this and
plan to avoid it.

"Knowledge is of no value unless you put it into
perspective." Anton Chekhov

# Uncertainty

There is much in life that is beyond our control
but much that is also predictable. For more certainty
in your life, learn to plan and in so doing feel
more at ease.

"Problems are a chance for us to do our best."
Duke Ellington

# Humour

Find out what or who makes you laugh. Double up on this person or situation as laughter is a powerful healer.

"The road to success is always under construction."
Lily Tomlin

# Motivation

With the right motivation, we can find the energy and belief to overcome what we doubted was possible.

"When we can no longer change a situation, we are challenged to change ourselves." Viktor Frankel

## Spirit/Determination

Those who are determined are not dispirited or disheartened for exceptionally long. To persist, find what galvanizes you. Find your unlosable cause.

"No thief can steal your will." Epicetus

# Releasing Tension

Releasing tension can transform your mood. Whether it is a movie that gets you enthralled or a show that gets you crying with laughter, build it in to your day.

"Regardless of how you feel inside always try to look a winner." Arthur Ashe

# Ocean Relief

Even on a cloudy day the sound of the breaking waves awakens the senses, whilst the crashing waves or even the calm waters rippling on the beach, soothe and caress our souls. Breathe in the fresh sea air whilst feeling the salinity of the ocean softening your skin. The ocean is a complete mental escape.

"Knock the 't' off the can't." Samuel Johnson

# Money

Money certainly makes life easier and lack of it can make for genuine frustration and difficulty. So, try and make what you value most, things that have nothing to do with money and better still, things that are in abundance. A hearty laugh, the morning sunrise, the first coffee of the day.

"Everything will be okay in the end. If it's not okay, it's not the end." John Lennon

# Negative Influences

Pay attention to who you spend time with. As unfair as it sounds, mixing with negative people will enhance your negativity. Alternatively, mixing with optimists will make you feel more positive.

"The search for happiness is one of the chief sources of unhappiness." Eric Hoffer

# Ioniser

Clean air just like drinking filtered water makes for a
more healthy and happy body and mind. Negative ions
are proven by research to enhance mental outlook.
Buy an air purifier.

"To him whom who is in fear, everything rustles."
Sophocles

# Modelling

Positive people appear relaxed and comfortable,
able to cope with the challenges they are facing.
Model yourself on them.

"Where the willingness is great the difficulties cannot
be great." Niccolo Machiavelli

# Leadership

Great leadership has inspired others to achieve things that seemed impossible. Read about some of the great leaders and get inspired.

"In all things it is better to hope than despair."
Wolfgang Von Goethe

# Lack Of!

Lack of anything creates a negative feeling in us because we are afraid, we will miss out. Even worse, the lack of certainty or uncertainty, is the biggest drain on positive emotions.

"To forgive is to set a person free and to discover the person was you." Louis B. Smedes

# Challenges Are Useful

Not everything is good all the time, how can it be?
How would we learn or appreciate what good even
meant? Accept that life's' challenges are what
ultimately make us stronger and happier and you
find sustained optimism.

"Do not pray for an easy life, pray for the strength
to endure a difficult one." Bruce Lee

# Planning

The only time we might genuinely enjoy uncertainty is with a surprise gift. A positive outlook stems from being able to manage to some degree, certainty in our lives. Plan one thing today that you wish to happen and feel your spirits rise.

"Nothing reduces the odds against you like ignoring them." Robert Breault

# Doubt

Challenges faced that we are not prepared for can cause doubt and bring about a crisis in confidence. Practice building emotional muscles. Take courses, read, and strive to learn vicariously from the challenges of others.

"Sometimes we're tested not to show our weaknesses but to discover our strengths." Anon

# Show The Love

When someone thanks you/shows appreciation for something you've done or for just being you, you feel good! Today, make a point of thanking someone for something perhaps, for being a great friend. This will enhance your friendship and give you a boost too.

"It's not the mountain we conquer but ourselves."
Edmund Hillary

# Engagement

When you are on a treadmill, rowing machine or lifting weights, most certainly actively engaged in competitive sport, you find an oasis from negativity.

"To be yourself in a world that's constantly trying to make you into somebody else is the greatest achievement." Ralph Waldo Emerson

# Quiet

A nearby park, a religious house of worship for peace if
not for prayer, a gallery, wherever you can find it, seek
an environment that provides respite from noise,
in and outside your head.

"The only difference between stumbling blocks and
stepping-stones is how you use them." Tom Sims

# Reading

Immerse yourself in a great novel. Be absorbed by the narrative of others and in so doing escape your own world whilst learning something new.

"Freedom is secured not by fulfillment of one's desires but by removal of desire." Epicetus

# Persistence

While you have the desire to keep going, while you persist you have belief or, positivity on steroids. Persist!

"Unless the vessel be pure everything which is poured into it will turn sour." Horace

# Rational Thinking

If what you wish for has a precedent, be very positive and know that your hearts' desire can be realized once more.

"Some people want it to happen, some wish it would happen, others make it happen." Michael Jordan

# Redemption

If you feel that things have not gone well, there is always tomorrow, even the rest of today is a chance to change things.

"Sometimes carrying on, just carrying on, is the superhuman achievement."   Albert Camus

# Healthy Body

A strong body with great circulation and even, easy breath, is one much more at ease with mental challenges. Requiring no special training, available to all and providing a sense of achievement, jog or simply walk for the sake of your body and mind.

"Some cause happiness wherever they go; Others whenever they go." Oscar Wilde

# Natural Light

SAD or Seasonal Affective Disorder negatively impacts
the mindsets of many and is caused by a lack
of sunlight. Either get some sun or eat leafy
vegetables, eggs or salmon!

"Beware the barrenness of a busy life."
Corrie Ten Boom

# Sleeping Like A Baby

Having a great nights' sleep makes you more capable
of fronting up to all the worlds' challenges.
Not sleeping well makes everything harder. Invest
in a mattress and pillows that effectively support
your head and body.

"Don't let the fear of striking out hold you back."
Babe Ruth

# Acceptance

Accepting who you are, knowing your strengths and
weaknesses, knowing that you are not perfect, as
you strive to do your best you will be a much
more content person.

"To succeed, jump as quickly at opportunities as you
do at conclusions."  Benjamin Franklin

# Weekend

Imagine that it is the weekend or a time when you are not compelled to work. You feel better already, right?

"Choose not to be harmed – and you won't be harmed – Don't feel harmed – and you haven't been." Marcus Aurelius

# Courage

Some of the challenges we must face can be or feel truly immense, but we face them anyway. It is courage that helps us to persist, to break through and being courageous now will make it easier the next time.

"What would you do if you weren't afraid?"
Sheryl Sandberg

# Multiple Challenges

Do not overburden yourself with multiple challenges at one time. A positive mind is one that anticipates progression, and this is more likely achieved when focusing on one thing.

"The water hollows out the stone, not by force but drop by drop." Lucretius

# Poetry

Thoughts, words, and actions can inspire us whilst poetry can help us imagine.

"Those who matter don't mind, and those who mind don't matter." Bernard Baruca

# Drink

Take a sip of your favorite drink and apart from feeling happier in an instant, your outlook will change to one of appreciation and with this thought, a more positive mindset.

"Success is getting up just one more time than you fall." Oliver Goldsmith

# Re-Energize

To relax, to mentally switch off, give your head and your body a break. Whether you put your feet up or have a long relaxing shower, find a way to energize.

"If you believe it will work out, you'll see opportunity. If you believe it won't you will see obstacles."
Wayne Dier

## Practice Makes Perfect

Practice optimism. Take a story with a bad outcome and automatically imagine the opposite ending. Take bad news and think what it would take for it to become good news. Focus on the positive. Build the mentality to default to optimism.

"We don't see things as they are, we see them as we are." Anais Nin

# Caring Acts

Today, call someone who you think could really do with hearing a familiar voice. Your voice. Make their day. You'll feel great!

"No one is useless in this world who lightens the burden of another." Charles Dickens

# Your Turn!

By now you will know that there are so many little
manageable steps that you can take. Try writing one
and send to: stuart@gettingpositivenow.com

So much of what happens in our lives feels way beyond our control. However, if you are proactive and take some small daily actions you will help nurture a more positive state of mind.

Inset, Stuart Parkin 'getting positive' by convening with nature and all its drama and beauty.

For an even more hopeful state of mind, go to: www. gettingpositivenow.com/ideas

Lightning Source UK Ltd.
Milton Keynes UK
UKHW010726130421
381918UK00003B/505

9 781839 754821